Lightning Bolt Books™

Scary Vampires

T0386292

Walt Brody

Lerner Publications • Minneapolis

Lerner Publications Company
An imprint of Lerner Publishing Group, Inc.
241 First Avenue North
Minneapolis, MN 55401 USA

For reading levels and more information, look up this title at www.lernerbooks.com.

Main body text set in Billy Infant regular.
Typeface provided by SparkType.

Library of Congress Cataloging-in-Publication Data

The Cataloging-in-Publication Data for *Scary Vampires* is on file at the Library of Congress.
ISBN 978-1-5415-9691-7 (lib. bdg.)
ISBN 978-1-72841-366-2 (pbk.)
ISBN 978-1-72840-051-8 (eb pdf)

Manufactured in the United States of America
1-47797-48237-12/23/2019

Table of Contents

What Is a Vampire?

Since the 1960s, people have thought Highgate Cemetery in London is the home of a vampire. Locals say something tall and pale with red eyes and sharp teeth attacks those passing by at night.

Stories say vampires have pointy fangs.

Many believe vampires were once humans who turned into monsters. Vampires are said to be strong, fast, and immortal (able to live forever). But they need blood to use their special abilities.

How do you destroy a vampire? One way, legend says, is to trick or trap a vampire into going out in the sun.

Nosferatu (1922) is one of the earliest films about vampires.

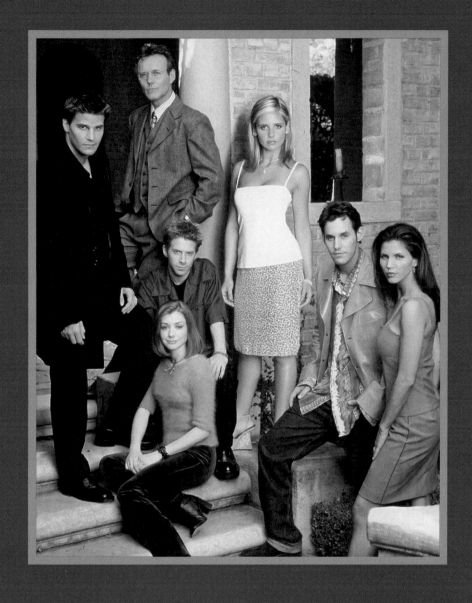

Many books, TV shows, and movies are about vampires. In the TV show *Buffy the Vampire Slayer* (1997-2003), vampires are evil.

History of Vampires

The story of Vlad III may be the first record of vampires. He lived in Transylvania between 1431 and 1476.

Vlad III was known as Vlad the Impaler.

Vlad III was a warrior who impaled his enemies. That means he pierced them with stakes.

Bram Stoker wrote *Dracula* in 1897. Some say it was based on Vlad III.

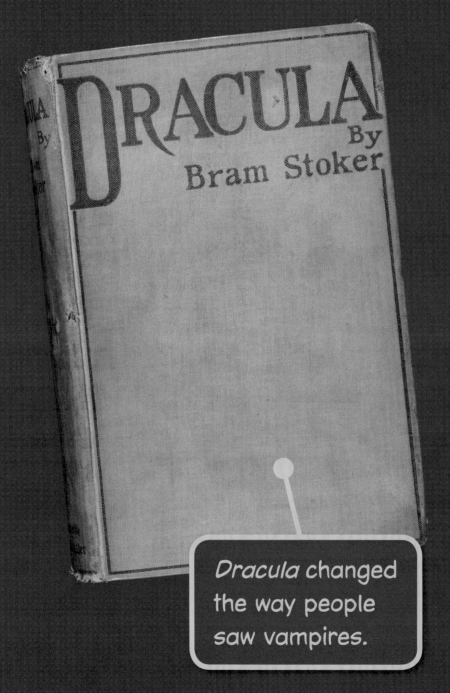

Dracula changed the way people saw vampires.

The book was about a vampire in Transylvania. Count Dracula became one of the most terrifying and famous monsters of all time.

Modern Vampires

Vampires are popular monsters. Many vampire fans wear dark makeup and clothes.

Some vampire fans wear fake fangs on their teeth to look more like vampires.

Some people even say they are real-life vampires. But they can't turn into bats, of course!

One real animal actually is a little like a vampire! It's the vampire bat. It drinks blood to survive.

Vampire bats drink mostly cattle blood.

Vampire bats cut into their prey with sharp teeth. That's how they got their name.

Are Vampires Real?

Vampires in movies have many special abilities, such as morphing, or changing into something else. In reality, those abilities do not exist.

Vlad III is commonly believed to be a prince.

Vlad III was a real person. But he was not immortal and was not really a vampire.

Vampire stories may be fun to read about. But there are no humanlike bloodsucking creatures.

Vampires can seem glamorous with their mysterious ways and dark clothes.

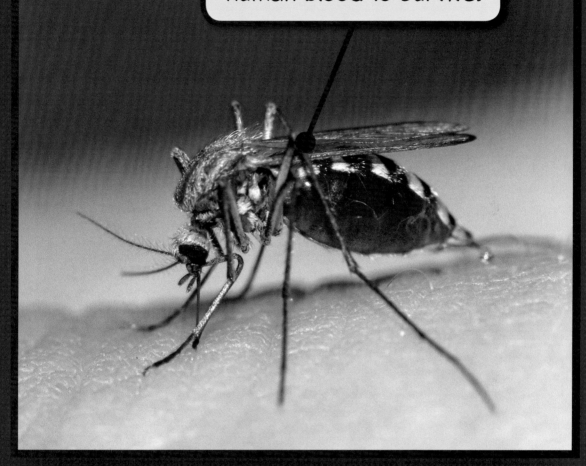

Mosquitoes drink human blood to survive.

Only animals such as mosquitoes can exist on blood alone. Thick clothing and screens can help keep these bloodsuckers away!

Close Encounter

More than 150 sheep were found drained of blood in India. Some people think hyenas could have done it. Others believe only a vampire could be the culprit.

Terrifying Trivia

- Vampires hate garlic. People might wear a necklace of garlic to protect themselves from a vampire.

- Vampires do not have reflections.

- Abraham Van Helsing is a character in Bram Stoker's *Dracula*. He hunted vampires and was Count Dracula's enemy.

Glossary

immortal: something that can live forever

impale: drive a spike through something

locals: people who live in an area

morphing: changing from one thing to another

prey: an animal that is eaten by another animal

stake: a wooden spike

Further Reading

Kiddle: Vampire Facts for Kids
https://kids.kiddle.co/Vampire

Kidzsearch: Vampire
https://wiki.kidzsearch.com/wiki/Vampire

Kidzworld: The Legend of Vampires
https://www.kidzworld.com/article/24861-the-legend-of-vampires

Lawrence, Sandra. *The Atlas of Monsters: Mythical Creatures from around the World*. Philadelphia: Running Press Kids, 2019.

Pearson, Maggie. *Ghosts and Goblins: Scary Stories from around the World*. Minneapolis: Darby Creek, 2016.

Shea, Therese M. *Bloodsucking Vampire Bats*. New York: Gareth Stevens, 2016.

Index

Photo Acknowledgments

Image credits: sherlesi/Shutterstock.com, p. 4; jsteck/Getty Images, p. 5; Hulton Archive/ Getty Images, p. 6; Marianna Ianovska/Shutterstock.com, p. 8; Stefano Bianchetti/ Corbis/Getty Images, p. 9; Held by British Library/Wikimedia Commons (Public Domain), p. 10; Universal Pictures/Getty Images, p. 11; pink_cotton_candy/E+/Getty Images, p. 12; jentakespictures/Getty Images, p. 13; Nathapol Kongseang/Shutterstock.com, p. 14; kyslynskahal/Shutterstock.com, p. 15; Dm_Cherry/Shutterstock.com, p. 16; LightRocket/ Getty Images, p. 17; ASHSTUDIO/Getty Images, p. 18; Pasi Koskela/Shutterstock.com, p. 19; iStockphoto/Getty Images, pp. 20, 22.

Cover: BirdHunter591/iStockphoto/Getty Images; Aleksey Boyko/Shutterstock.com; MerlinTmb/Shutterstock.com.